1,000 Marks

1,000 Marks
by Pentagram

Since it was founded in 1972 by graphic designers Alan Fletcher, Colin Forbes and Mervyn Kurlansky, architect Theo Crosby and industrial designer Kenneth Grange, Pentagram has always been a multidisciplinary design agency – however, creating brand identities for clients from many different industries and continents is the biggest part of what Pentagram does.

The humble mark is central to all of these well-honed brand identities. Also known as the logo, logotype, symbol or wordmark, marks often act as shorthand for the brand itself. Marks are everywhere – they enter our collective psyche, they're part of the cultural landscape and they symbolise the relationships we form with brands.

The 1,000 marks featured in this book represent the diverse range of identity work created by Pentagram partners past and present. For more than 50 years, Pentagram has designed marks for everyone from multinational corporations to start-ups, government agencies, nonprofits and social enterprises, clubs, societies, individuals, districts and even whole countries. Regardless of your identity, an original mark that you can take ownership of is the starting point for communicating who you are and what you do.

While things have certainly moved on in recent years, with 3D, motion and flexible identities opening up a world of opportunities for brand expression, a memorable and expertly crafted mark that embodies the essence of the brand lies at the heart of any meaningful brand identity. Marks have to work very hard these days – they need to function equally well as a tiny icon in a social media app, while still looking good on a giant digital billboard. They also need to present well in monochrome, in colour, as flat, in three dimensions and when animated.

There are many approaches to creating a distinctive logo, and all of them can be seen here, from bold typographic wordmarks to pictorial symbols and more abstract solutions. Printing them in black and white helps us see them in their purest form, highlighting the contrasts and occasional similarities between them.

The practice of design has changed radically since 1972, but its concerns remain the same. The deceptively simple exercise of designing a mark for a client, and the elusive quest for timelessness that it entails, are still central to the challenge that graphic designers face today.

A More Perfect Union 2021
The Philadelphia Inquirer's year-long investigation into
the roots of systemic racism in the United States

AA Ligature 2021
Signet for the Architectural Association London

AA Visiting School 2022
Visiting School of the Architectural Association London

_able 2017
Investment partnership with a focus on women-led
brands in the healthy-living space

Academy of Achievement 1991
Not-for-profit foundation that puts young people
in contact with America's achievers

Academy Museum 2021
Cultural destination for the Academy of Motion Picture
Arts and Sciences based in Los Angeles, California

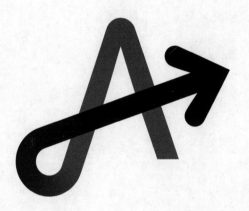

Achieve 2021
Personal financial-service platform

Abu Dhabi Sports 2017
Sports TV channel in the United Arab Emirates

ADAM KATZ SINDING

Adam Katz Sinding 2019
Logotype for photographer Adam Katz Sinding

ADWEEK

Adweek 2011
Weekly magazine for the advertising industry

Aephea

Aephea 2023
Private residential real estate portfolio

Affinity 2015
Digital-driven financial institution in Ghana

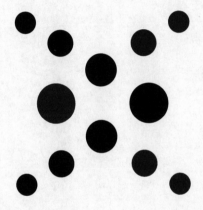

Afinis 2018
Electronic payments association

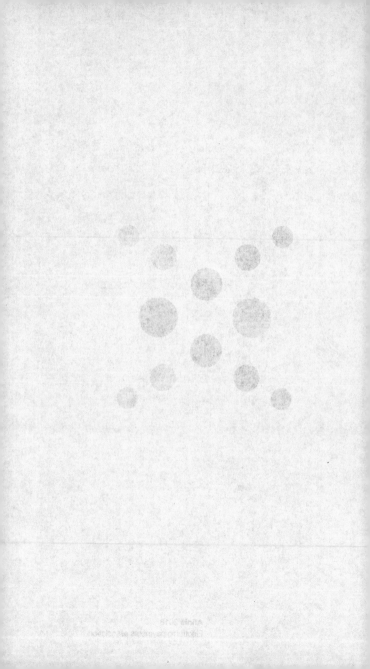

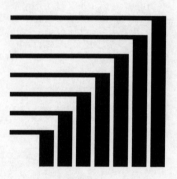

Aga Khan Fund for Economic Development 1986
Charitable foundation

AGBO 2019
Independent entertainment company founded
by Anthony and Joe Russo

AIA Design Revolution 2011
American Institute of Architects 2011
National Convention and Design Exposition
in New Orleans, Louisiana

AIG 2012
International insurance and financial organisation

Air AA 2020
Architectural Association London podcast

Airlines for America 2011
Trade association of the principal US airlines

Airlines for Europe 2020
Not-for-profit organisation representing major
European airlines in Brussels, Belgium

AirTrain 1998
Light-rail system that links New York's airports
to its mass-transit systems

The Al Thani Collection 2020
Private art collection

Albertine 2014
French-language bookstore at the Consulate General
of France in New York City

L'Alliance

L'Alliance

L'Alliance 2024
Non-profit organisation that promotes French
and Francophone culture and language through
educational and artistic programmes

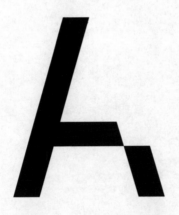

Alloyed 2020
Company providing digital solutions
for metal components

Almaty Financial District 2007
International financial centre in Almaty, Kazakhstan

Alpages 2016
Online shop selling high-quality Swiss cheese in the UK

AITi

ALVARIUM

Alvarium Investments 2019
Global wealth and asset management

Amalgamated Bank 2013
Largest union-owned bank in the United States

AMANDA WAKELEY

Amanda Wakeley 2000
London couture designer

Ambigram 2008
Greek advertising agency

ambre

Ambre 2012
Four-star resort on the east coast of Mauritius

American Folk Art Museum 2000
Museum of traditional American folk art and crafts

HQRSE

American Quarter Horse Association 2001
Quarter Horse breed registry and
membership organisation

American Express 2017
International financial services company

American Girl

American Girl 2023
Doll company using American history and storytelling
to empower girls with confidence

American Weed Co. 2023
Veteran-owned cannabis brand

Amherst College 2018
Prestigious liberal arts college in Massachusetts

Andy Warhol Black & White
Andy Warhol Black & White

Andy Warhol Black & White 2010
Exhibition of black-and-white paintings by the artist
at the Prism Gallery in Los Angeles, California

ANGLE

Angle Theatre 2009
Commissioning charity for new theatre playwrights

ankorstore

Ankorstore 2022
Online wholesaler connecting independent
brands and retailers

ANYDAY

ANYDAY 2021
Own-brand product range for John Lewis

Appy Fizz 2022
India's leading sparkling apple juice

April Housing 2022
Affordable housing portfolio company

April 🌸

Archewell 2020
International non-profit advocacy organisation
founded by the Duke and Duchess of Sussex

Archtober 2011
Month-long festival of architecture and design
in New York City

Arian 2020
Printing and campaign-planning company in Austria

Art Institute of Chicago 2008
World-renowned art museum founded in 1879

Art Republic 2022
Online art retailer

ArtCenter

Art Center College of Design 1988
Art and design school in Pasadena, California

Art UK 2013
UK-based charity and online platform providing
access to all publicly owned art

ARUP

Arup 1985
International civil engineering consultancy

As iFF 2015
Yearly film festival by the Hudson River that focuses
on short films

Asea Brown Boveri 1987
Multinational engineering company with operations
in over 100 countries

Asia Society 1997
Dedicated to fostering an understanding
of and communication between Americans
and the peoples of the Asia-Pacific region

The Asian American Foundation 2021
The first and largest advocacy institution
for Asian Americans in the United States

Asprey

Asprey 2002
Quintessentially British luxury goods brand
founded in 1781

The Atheneum 1990
Luxury hotel in the Greektown area
of Detroit, Michigan

Atlantic Theater 2015
Theatre showcasing original plays that go
onto Broadway

*the*Atlantic

The Atlantic 2008
One of America's oldest monthly magazines

auros

Auros Home 2023
Home customisation platform for homeowners
and builders

Aviv Clinics 2019
Hyperbaric oxygen therapy centres

Axess 2022
Mass-market credit card for Turkish bank, Akbank

axis

Axis 2022
Cloud-based cybersecurity platform based
in Tel Aviv, Israel

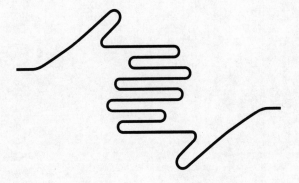

B2B Equality 2000
Electronic information exchange for start-up
companies and entrepreneurs

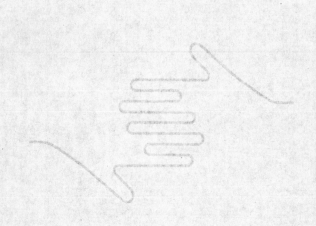

Bach 2000
Festival of classical music by the German composer

THE BAFFLER

The Baffler 2015
Literary magazine tweaking established dogma
in politics, economics, art and culture

Baltimore Center Stage 2016
Performing arts venue based in Baltimore, Maryland

Bankside 2014
Logo and flag for Bankside London

BankUnited 2010
Bank with more than ninety branch locations
in thirteen Florida counties

Baret Scholars 2023
Immersive global gap-year experience
for high school graduates

Barnes Foundation 2012.
All rights reserved. No part of this document
may be reproduced without permission.

Barnes Foundation 2012
Art museum and educational resource
in Philadelphia, Pennsylvania

Batcow 2011
Public art installation sponsored by Austin CowParade

Battersea Pie Station 2008
Cafés specialising in classic London pie and mash

bʌuhʌus ʌrchiv

Bauhaus-Archiv 2014
Archive and design museum

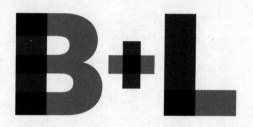

Bausch + Lomb 2010
One of the biggest healthcare brands in the world

Beacon 1999
Restaurant built around a huge, hearth-like wood-
burning oven in Manhattan, New York

Ben's Best Blnz 2022
Cannabis brand investing 100% of profits back into
the Black cannabis community and groups advocating
for criminal justice reform

Bennington College

Bennington College 2023
Storied liberal and fine arts college
in Bennington, Vermont

Berkeley Rep 2020
Repertory theatre located in Berkeley, California

THE BERKELEY

Berry Bros. & Rudd 2012
Britain's oldest wine merchants

Bertazzoni 2005
Family-owned Italian manufacturer of professional-style cooking ranges

Beverly Willis Architecture Foundation 2020
Non-profit recognising the role of women
in architecture and engineering

bicycle

Bicycle 2021
Real-time insights and operations platform

Big Ten Conference 2010
Oldest and largest US Division I college
athletic association

The Big Draw 2011
Annual event for The Campaign for Drawing

The Big Issue 2021
World's most widely circulated street newspaper

Bike New York 2015
Not-for-profit organisation that promotes
and encourages bicycling and bicycle safety

Birds of Prey 2020
American film based on the DC Comics character
Harley Quinn

BitStreams 2002
Exhibition of digital artwork held at the Whitney
Museum of American Art

Black Box Theater 2008
Theatre at the Maryland Institute College
of Art, Baltimore

Black Focus Records 2022
Electronic and jazz record label

Blood Cancer UK 2020
UK-based charity dedicated to funding research
for and raising awareness of all blood cancers

BLOODS

Bloods 2021
British television sitcom created by Samson Kayo
and Nathan Bryon, produced by Roughcut Television

BLOODS

Book of Kells Experience 2023
Digital experience for the Book of Kells in Trinity
College, Dublin, Ireland

Bookshop.org

Bookshop 2022
Online bookseller donating profits to a group
of existing small bookstores

Boulevard Las Vegas 2021
Multi-use entertainment destination
on the Las Vegas strip

BPF Capital 2023
Family investment firm enabling sustainable
management of generational wealth

Braunschweig International Film Festival 2020
Film festival of the city of Braunschweig, Germany

Breaking the Ice 2005
International not-for-profit organisation that seeks
to transform conflicts into trust and mutual respect

Bridges 2007
Capital campaign for the Judah L. Magnes Museum
of Jewish Culture

BROAD ART MUSEUM

Broad Art Museum 2012
Contemporary art museum designed by Zaha Hadid
at Michigan State University

Broadway Books 1995
Division of Bantam Doubleday Dell named after the
thoroughfare that bisects the street grid in Manhattan,
New York

Brooklyn Academy of Music 1995
Venue for avant-garde performing arts

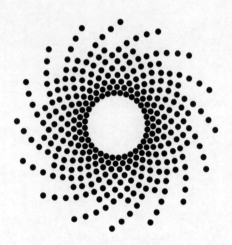

Brooklyn Historical Society 2003
Institution dedicated to the appreciation of New York
City's most populous borough

the
Bruce

Bruce 2022
Museum of art and science in Greenwich, Connecticut

BRUNSWICK

Brunswick 2004
Corporate communications advisors

BuddhaBerry

BuddhaBerry 2023
Frozen yoghurt shop based in Sag Harbor, New York

Buffy

Buffy 2017
Eco-friendly bedding company dedicated
to sustainable comfort and quality

Builder

Builder 2011
Magazine for the home-building industry

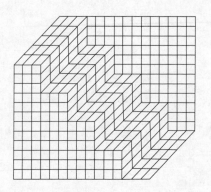

Buro Happold 1977
International structural engineering firm

BXP 2016
Real estate investment firm whose stock
symbol is BXP

CAFE ROYAL

CAFÉ ROYAL

Café Royal 2012
Renewed as a five-star hotel in the West End
of London

Caledonian MacBrayne 2021
Scottish Western Isles ferry service

California Academy of Sciences 2007
Science institution housing a museum, planetarium
and aquarium

California State University, Chico 2021
Public university in Chico, California

Callaway Golf 2000
Manufacturer of golfing equipment

Câm 2022
Company set up to produce, distribute and sell fresh,
pasteurised milk throughout Nigeria

Cambridge Quantum

Cambridge Quantum 2020
Software company for quantum computers

Camden Art Centre
Arkwright Road
London NW3

Canal & River Trust 2011
UK national waterways charity

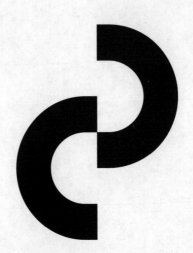

Capital Partners 2006
International real estate development firm

Caprice 2016
German shoe manufacturer

Carbyne 2021
Software company developing cloud-based
mission-critical contact centre solutions

Cardless

Cardless 2020
Platform for consumer brands to launch
credit card products

Carl 2019
High-rise building made from timber

Carnegie Center 2017
Technology and medical campus

Cass Art 2003
London-based chain of art-supply stores

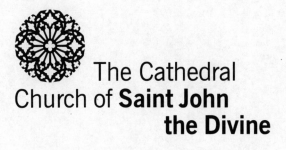

The Cathedral Church of **Saint John the Divine**

The Cathedral Church of Saint John the Divine 2013
Historic Episcopal church on New York City's Upper
West Side

REYNOLDS

**Catherine B. Reynolds Foundation
Program in Social Entrepreneurship** 2006
New York University programme that trains the
next generation of public service leaders

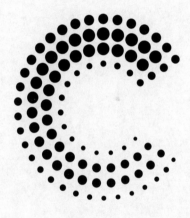

Cazana 2021
Platform providing data insights for the
automotive industry, based in the UK

Celebration, Florida 1993
New Urbanist community near Orlando, Florida

Center for Architecture 2001
Public centre dedicated to New
York and the built environment

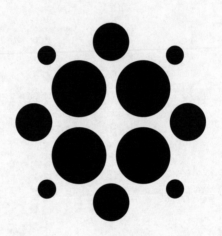

CFP Energy 2023
Energy and environmental solutions provider

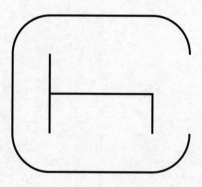

Chambers Hotel 2001
Boutique hotel in Midtown Manhattan
with a Downtown aesthetic, New York

CHANNELSIDE

Channelside 2020
Waterfront commercial and civic centre

ChaShaMa

ChaShaMa 2016
Nonprofit providing affordable studios
and performance venues for artists

chaucer

Chaucer 2020
Global specialty (re)insurance group

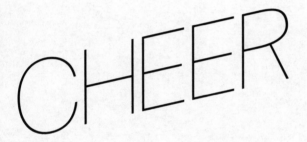

Cheer 2020
American television docuseries following
the Navarro College cheerleading team

Chicken Now 2009
Fast-food chain located exclusively in shopping mall
food courts

Chicken & Egg Films 2023
Supporters of women and non-binary filmmakers

Chicory 2023
Hotel in Seoul, South Korea

China Europe Creative 2012
Chinese-Austrian cultural collaboration

China Max 2011
Chinese fast-food restaurant chain

Chris Carey Advisors

Chris Carey Advisors 2013
Strategic business consultants

CHRYSLER BUILDING

Chrysler Museum of Art 2023
Art museum in Norfolk, Virginia

the CHURCHILL fellowship

The Churchill Fellowship 2020
UK charity investing in social change

CHUS X CHUS

Chus x Chus 2017
Jewellery line by internationally renowned designer
Chus Burés

CINDY CHAO

Cindy Chao 2022
Jewellery brand

Citi 2000
World's largest financial institution

Citizen

Citizen 2021
Magazine exploring Black culture and creativity

City University of New York 2004
America's largest urban public university

CITYPOINT

City Point 2017
Civic centre in Brooklyn, New York

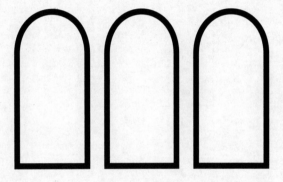

Civic Campus 2021/2022
Old town hall remodelled into a multi-function
hub and meeting place in the London Borough
of Hammersmith and Fulham

Claridge's

Claridge's 1995
Historic five-star London society hotel

Classical.com 2001
Online classical music retailer

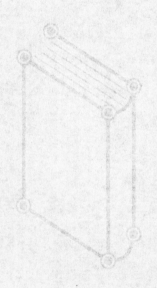

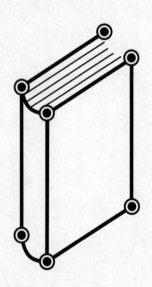

Classmap 2000
Online class notes, curriculum and schedules

The Cleveland Orchestra 2023
American orchestra

CloudShield 2001
Computer network security company

CO2FILM

CO2FILM 2015
Film production company based in Berlin, Germany

COCORICO

codecademy

Codecademy 2016
World's largest online platform offering free coding
and programming education

Coefficient Capital

Coefficient Capital 2019
Early-stage venture capital firm

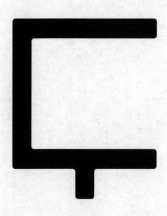

Coeuraj 2021
Management consulting firm in Montreal, Canada

Cohere 2021
Canadian multinational technology company
focused on AI for enterprise, specialising in large
language models

COLGATE

Colgate University 2019
Private liberal arts college in Hamilton, New York

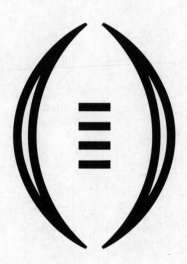

College Football National Championship 2014
American collegiate football playoffs
and championship

COLORS

COLORS Magazine 2004
Multilingual international magazine published
by Benetton

COLORS

Columbia Business School 2007
Graduate school of business at Columbia University

Commercial Bank of Kuwait 1980
Consumer and corporate bank founded in 1960

THE
COMMISSION
ON
PRESIDENTIAL
DEBATES

The Commission on Presidential Debates 2020
Non-partisan sponsors of American general election
presidential debates

THE CONDUCTOR

The Conductor 2021
Documentary on Marin Alsop, the first female
conductor of a major American symphony

THE CONRAN SHOP.
T   C   S   .

CONTEMPORARY JEWISH MUSEUM

Contemporary Jewish Museum 2007
Museum that explores contemporary perspectives
on Jewish culture, history, art and ideas, based in
San Francisco, California

The Contemporary Austin

The Contemporary Austin 2013
Contemporary art museum in Austin, Texas

COOPER HEWITT

Cooper Hewitt 2014
Smithsonian Design Museum located in New York City
housing one of the most diverse and comprehensive
design collections in the world

COQODAQ 2023
Korean fried chicken restaurant in New York City

COQUAL

Coqual 2021
Global think tank and advisory group focused
on workplace diversity, equity and inclusion

Coram 2000
The UK's oldest children's charity

Corella Publishing 2006
Producer of illustrated books and documentaries

Corigin 2010
Urban planning and investment firm

Cornell Lab of Ornithology 2008
Identity based on the work of wildlife artist Charley
Harper for an institute whose mission is to interpret
and conserve the earth's biodiversity

Cornerstone 2021
Cloud-based HR solutions company

Corridor 2010
Urban real estate development firm

Cote 2017
Michelin-starred Korean barbecue steakhouse
in New York City

Council of Fashion Designers of America 1992
Not-for-profit trade association for designers
of fashion and fashion accessories

County Highway 2023
News and culture publication in the form
of a nineteenth-century newspaper

Courts at Birch Meadows 2002
Tennis club in Greenwich, Connecticut

Coutts |

Coutts 2018
Private banking and wealth management

covariant

Covariant 2019
AI robotics company developing a universal AI,
enabling robots to see, reason and act on the
world around them

Crafts Council 2020
UK national craft charity

Cranks 2022
Coffee shop and bicycle workshop

Cranks Cycling Club 2022
Cycling club and workshop

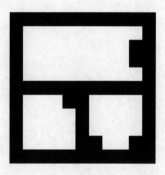

Creative Land Trust 2019
Funding studio space in London for creatives

Crestline 2011
Hedge fund management firm located
in Fort Worth, Texas

The Crimes of Grindelwald 2018
Second instalment in the Fantastic Beasts
film franchise

The Criterion Collection 2006
Publishers of classic and contemporary
cinema on DVD

Crocus 2000
Online garden centre

Crossroads Films 1989
Film production company

Crouch End Festival Chorus

Crouch End Festival Chorus 2013
One of Britain's leading symphonic choirs

Crown Dispensaries 2019
Cannabis company based in Los Angeles, California

Culture Mile 2017
Cultural and creative hub in London's Square Mile

curiouspictures

Curious Pictures 1993
Mixed media, live action, animation and computer
graphics studio

Cytora

Cytora 2018
Configurable platform that enables commercial
insurers to process risks at greater efficiency
and accuracy

Daishin 2010
Financial investment company

Dallas Opera 1978
Performing arts company

Dallas Arboretum and Botanical Garden 2013
One of the top three arboretums in the United States

Dally

Dally 2019
Premium line of botanical hand-wash soaps

Damiani 2001
Luxury jewellery brand based in Milan, Italy

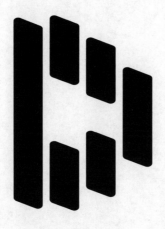

Dashlane 2018
World's leading personal identity and password
management system

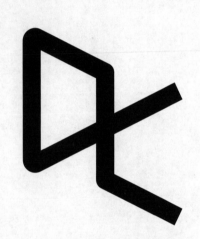

Datacamp 2020
Data and AI educational company aimed
at democratising data skills

dataland

Dataland 2023
Museum focused on new media and data art

Dataland 2.2.8
M sh' Ahtha'usa'ly w mile s rod Ala' of

DC Entertainment 2016
American entertainment company dedicated
to DC Comics' characters and stories

Doha Exhibition and Conference Center 2019
Exhibition and conference centre in Qatar

Dehesa Gago 2000
Fine Spanish wine produced by Telmo Rodriguez

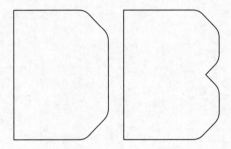

Della Valle Bernheimer 2007
Contemporary architecture firm based
in New York City

Delta Faucet Company 2001
Manufacturer of domestic and commercial faucets

Design Declares 2022
Industry group committed to tackling
the climate emergency

Design Frontiers

Design Frontiers 2017
Group exhibition, telling the stories of sustainable
projects, products and initiatives

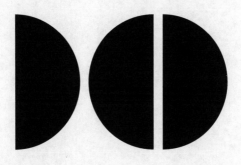

Design Objectives 1972
Manufacturing and marketing company

Design Village 2020
Annual design conference in Ivano-Frankivsk, Ukraine

Destiny Villa 2015
Private villa in Montego Bay, Jamaica

Detroit Institute of Arts 2006
Fine arts museum founded in 1885

The Devonshire Group 2024
Holding group for businesses and charities throughout
the UK and Ireland

The Devonshire Group – Chatsworth House 2024
Stately home in Derbyshire, UK

Dick Bruna Huis 2005
Permanent collection celebrating the work of the
creator of Miffy, housed at the Centraal Museum
in Utrecht, the Netherlands

Dick Clark Productions 2023
Iconic American television production company

Dietz Connect 2019
Media and journalism consultant

Digital Architecture Lab 2022
Innovation lab focused on web3
and digital transformation

Digital Turbine 2022
International advertising technology company

DK 2020
International publishing company

DMAT - SDMI 1999
International consortium of digital music
and technology companies

DIRIYAH

DIRIYAH

Diriyah 2019
Destination brand for Diriyah City, built around
the UNESCO world heritage site of At-Turaif

الدرعية

Documenta Archiv 2017
Archive related to the contemporary
art fair Documenta

DOKUARTS

DOKUARTS 2018
German film festival for documentary films
on the subject of art

DOMAINE-THOMSON

Domaine-Thomson 2015
Family-run wine producers in New Zealand and France

Don't Tell Anyone 2023
Podcast hosted by Imane Anys, an entrepreneur,
social-media personality and Twitch streamer

Donovan Bar 2018
London bar dedicated to photographer
Terence Donovan

The Dorchester

Dorchester Collection 2006
Worldwide portfolio of five-star hotels

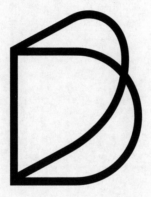

Dosde 2018
Spanish leading publishing house that specialises
in books on art, architecture, cities and travel

Drake's

Drake's 2011
Contemporary gentlemen's haberdasher

DRYSTONE

CHAMBERS

Drystone Chambers 2015
Leading London-based criminal chambers

DSTLRY 2023
Next-generation comics publisher that redefines
creator-owned comic books and collectibles

Dusit Central Park 2019
Mixed-use skyscraper development in the Bang Rak
district of Bangkok, Thailand

Dusit Thani 2018
Thai multinational hospitality company headquartered
in Bangkok, Thailand

Dwarfs and Giants 2015
Business consultancy based in Vienna, Austria

EASTBANK

EastBank 2019
Cultural quarter at the heart of Queen Elizabeth
Olympic Park, London

EAT ŎFFBEAT

Eat Offbeat 2020
New York City-based social impact food
company offering cuisine created by former
refugees turned chefs

EAT OFFBEAT

EAT.

Eclipse 2006
Lost, forgotten or overshadowed film classics from
The Criterion Collection

Editions de l'Olivier 1991
French publishing house

Editions Payot 1988
French publishing house

EDP 2022
Largest energy company in Portugal and a global
leader in the renewable energy sector

EIGEN HUIS & INTERIEUR

Eigen Huis & Interieur 2012
Design and interiors magazine based in Amsterdam,
the Netherlands

$\frac{18}{82}$

1837

1837 1998
Restaurant at Brown's Hotel in Mayfair, London

1837

Electra 2000
European private equity investors

Electronic Frontier Foundation 2018
Non-profit organisation defending civil liberties
in the digital world

Elektra Entertainment 1989
American record label

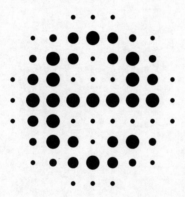

Elephant 2020
Healthcare operating system

Eli and Edythe Broad Art Museum 2012
Zaha Hadid-designed contemporary art museum
at Michigan State University

Emerald City Press 2007
Coffee, news and flower shop in Austin, Texas

END.

END.

END. 2012
Men's clothing brand

EndemolShine

Endo at the Rotunda 2019
Michelin-starred sushi restaurant in London

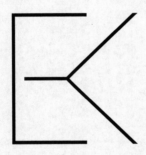

Endo Kazutoshi 2019
Third-generation sushi master

Ennovate 2021
Global innovation hub

Entain 2021
International sports and gaming group

EQL 2022
Financial health platform in the United States

ERM 2023
World's largest advisory firm focused solely
on sustainability

ESPA

Espa 2005
Luxury spa products, treatments and design

ESPRIT

ESPRIT 2019
Iconic fashion brand known for its casual style
and youthful spirit

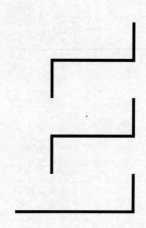

Essenziale 2007
Lingerie and swimwear boutique in Mayfair, London

ESTĒE LAUDER

Estée Lauder 1994
Manufacturer and marketer of skincare, makeup,
fragrance and haircare products

EUREKA!

Eureka! 1987
Children's museum

EUREKA

Eureka 2023
Showcase of design-led innovation from the UK's
leading research centres

Eurosport 2015
Pan-European television sports network

Eva 1981
Lithographic printer

EVERNOW

Evernow 2021
Digital healthcare platform specialising in women's
health and menopause-related conditions

Expedia Group 2018
Hotel-booking corporation

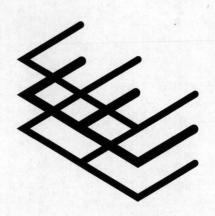

Exponent 2017
Private equity firm

FABRIANO

Fabriano 2021
Iconic Italian paper manufacturer

Faber & Faber 1981
Independent literary publishing house

Faber Music 1981
Sheet music division of Faber & Faber

facult*y*

Faculty 2018
Applied AI consultancy and technology in the UK

FAENA

Faena 2012
Premium hospitality in Miami, Florida and Buenos
Aires, Argentina

Fantastic Beasts and Where to Find Them 2016
Prequel film to the Harry Potter book and film series

The Fashion Center 1993
Business improvement district encouraging the
development of New York City's Garment District

FASHION GOOD FOR

Fashion for Good 2018
Global initiative in sustainability for the fashion industry

FASHION FRINGE

Fashion Fringe 2006
Finding and supporting the next generation of British
fashion designers

Fashion Law Institute 2010
Centre at New York City's Fordham University that
advises designers and lawyers in areas of the law
affecting the fashion industry

Fashion Institute of Technology 2012
Athletics programme for the New York City-
based school

Fast Ed 1999
Software training company

Fifteen Fifteen by Ole Scheeren 2020
Residential building in Vancouver, Canada

FIFTY THREE

FIFTY  THREE

53 2022
Elevated modern Asian cuisine underneath
MoMA's new wing

FiLM iNDEP ENDENT SPiRiT AWARDS

Film Independent Spirit Awards 2016
Annual award ceremony dedicated to independent film

Fine Line Features 1991
Film production company

Finest[★]

Tesco Finest 1998
Premium range of food and drink for Tesco

FIRST THINGS

First Things 2017
Educational institute aiming to advance a religiously
informed public philosophy

Fisher-Price 2019
American toy company that creates fun and inspiring
toys dedicated to a child's development

Five Franklin Place 2008
Condominium residences in New York City

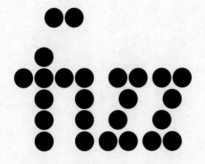

Fizz 2001
Healthcare marketing company

Flash:Light

Flash:Light 2011
Public arts festival in New York City

Flatiron/23rd Street Partnership 2007
Business improvement district in New York City
surrounding the intersection of Fifth Avenue,
23rd Street and Broadway

FLATIRON NOMAD

Flatiron NoMad 2022
Business development district centred at the
intersection of Broadway and Fifth Avenue in
Manhattan, New York

FLOUR AND SALT

Flour and Salt Bakery 2016
Market-style bakery based in Taipei

Flow Gallery 2014
Modern gallery representing makers working
with ceramics, glass, paper, wood, textiles, metal
and jewellery

FM&V

FM&V 2019
Agency and distribution arm of Berry Bros. & Rudd

Folio:

Folio 2001
Publishing industry news magazine

Folk Music Hall of Fame and Museum 2016
Music institution

Forgotten Architects 2014
Association dedicated to all German Jewish
architects banned by Nazi Germany

Fort Worth Museum of Science and History 2009
Science and history museum located in Fort
Worth, Texas

Fortuny 2021
Printed fabric company based in Venice, Italy

Fortuny Design Labs 2014
Design studio of the Fortuny fabrics company

450 Park Avenue 2007
Iconic black granite office tower in Manhattan,
New York City

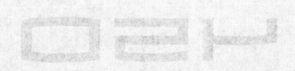

Fox River Paper 1988
American paper manufacturer

frankfurt

Frankfurt 2004
City of Frankfurt, Germany

THE FRICK COLLECTION

The Frick Collection 2024
Art museum and library focused on painting,
sculpture and decorative arts

FRIEZE

Frieze 2021
International modern and contemporary
art magazine and fair

FROOTI

Frooti 2015
Indian mango-flavoured fruit drink

FROST SCIENCE

Frost Science 2017
Children's science museum in Miami, Florida

fruufruit

fruitful

Fruitful 2022
Financial wellness platform

fuigo

Fuigo 2015
Interior design technology and coworking space

galaxy

Galaxy 2022
Institutional advisory firm specialising
in cryptocurrency investments

Galleria Colonna 1990
Italian shopping and business centre

GARDEN MUSEUM

Garden Museum 2016
London museum celebrating the art, history
and design of gardens

GATO

Gato 2014
Mediterranean restaurant in New York City
by chef Bobby Flay

Gebrüder Heinemann 1975
Distribution, logistics and a chain of retail stores
for the international travel industry

G!

Geronimo Inns 2003
Gastropubs in London and the south-east
of England

getronics

Getronics 2021
End-to-end digital transformation partner

gettyimages

Getty Images 2000
Stock photography library

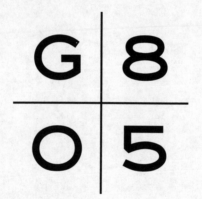

Giudecca 805 2013
Fortuny fabrics product brand

Global Design Forum 2013
London Design Festival's curated thought leadership
programme, celebrating design and the minds
shaping its future

GLUCK+

Gluck+ 2011
New York City contemporary architecture firm

Glyphs 2020
Complete font editor for drawing type

GolfDigest

Golf Digest 2014
Recreational and competitive golf magazine

GOLLA 2007
Producer of high-resolution transmission
electron microscopes

The Good Diner 1992
Traditional American diner in New York City

good dog

Good Dog 2018
Digital platform that connects high-quality dog
breeders, shelters and rescues with potential owners

Gotham Equities 1992
New York City real estate development firm

GOV/ART/COL

Gov/Art/Col 2019
UK government art collection

grace farms

Grace Farms 2012
Social and cultural institution in New Canaan,
Connecticut fostering community, pursuing social
justice and exploring the connections between art,
nature and faith

Gradient Learning 2020
Non-profit organisation focused on the holistic
education for students and teachers

Granary Associates 1995
Architecture and engineering firm based
in Philadelphia, Pennsylvania

Grand Central Terminal 2012
Identity based on the iconic clock in the New York
City rail station, with hands pointing to 19:13 for the
year of its founding

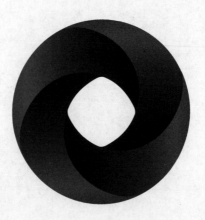

Graphcore 2017
UK-based semiconductor company that develops
accelerators for AI and machine learning

Great Jones 2019
New York City-based direct-to-consumer
cookware brand

Great Western Railway 2015
Iconic UK railway network designed by Isambard
Kingdom Brunel

Green Africa 2019
Nigerian airline based in Lagos, Nigeria

GREEN-WOOD

Green-Wood 2024
Historic cemetery with educational and cultural
programming in Brooklyn, New York

Green Canteen 2008
Restaurant that offers locally sourced and
environmentally friendly dishes in Brooklyn,
New York

The Guardian

The Guardian 1988
UK national newspaper

GUGGENHEIM

Guggenheim 2024
Constellation of museums in Venice, New York City,
Bilbao and Abu Dhabi

GUILDHALL SCHOOL

Guildhall School of Music & Drama 2014
Elite school of performing arts in London

gush

Gush 2023
Odourless & VOC-free paint, purifying pollutants
for healthier indoor spaces

Gutsy 2023
Process mining company helping businesses
with security governance

Hafen Offenbach 2006
Property development project in Offenbach, Germany

halfords

Halfords 2001
Retailer of bicycles, car care products,
parts and accessories

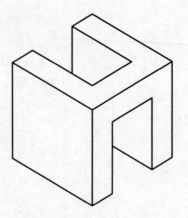

Halstead 2019
Leading New York City residential real estate
brokerage firm

Hammerson 2015
Prime urban real estate owners and operators

Handel
& Hendrix
in London

Handel & Hendrix in London 2014
Museum in Mayfair, London dedicated to George
Frideric Handel and Jimi Hendrix

Happy Face Pizza 2018
Retro-chic Neapolitan pizzeria in London

Happy Valley Meat Co. 2020
Sustainable meat company connecting farmers
to Michelin-starred restaurants

Harambeans 2018
Pioneering platform that inspires innovation ventures
and social change across Africa

Harmony Extracts 2016
Cannabis concentrate company

HARTBEAT

Hartbeat 2022
Kevin Hart's global media company dedicated
to the intersection of comedy and culture

HAY
FESTIVAL

Hay Festival 2019
One of the world's biggest literature festivals,
founded in Hay-on-Wye, Wales, UK

HEALGEL®

HealGel 2011
Skincare brand

HEAL'S

Heal's 2005
Retailers of contemporary furniture and homeware

Healthcare Realty Trust 2008
Real estate investment trust that develops doctor's
offices and medical pavilions

HealthClicks 2019
App platform that simplifies healthcare
facility compliance

Heart Center 1979
Clinic for cardiological disorders

Heart and Stroke 2016
Canada's national heart disease organisation

Hemasafe 1995
Autologous blood bank franchise

HEMISPHERES

Hemispheres 1992
United Airlines in-flight magazine

Henn na Hotel

NEW YORK

Henn na Hotel 2015
New York City hotel and spa

Hennepin Arts 2024
Non-profit arts trust organisation based
in Minneapolis, Minnesota

Heritage Radio Network 2020
US public radio network about cooking and cuisine

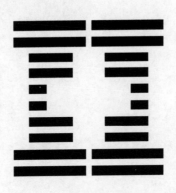

Hermann Hospital 1989
Part of the Texas Medical Centre in Houston, Texas

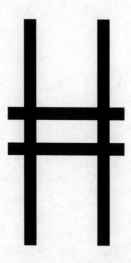

The High Line 2001
New York City's iconic railway-turned-park

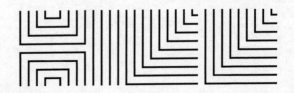

Hill Art Foundation 2019
Public exhibition and education space
in New York City

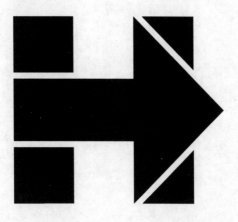

Hillary for America 2016
Hillary Rodham Clinton's 2016 presidential campaign

Hipgnosis 2022
Design agency formed by Po Powell
and Storm Thorgerson

HMBradley

HMBradley 2019
Digital banking platform that rewards people
for positive financial behaviors

Hologram

Hologram 2021
Health and wellness company focused
on personalised nutrition solutions

Hood Museum of Art 2020
Art museum and teaching resource on the campus
of Dartmouth College in New Hampshire

HOTSHOT 2016
Sports drink that prevents and treats muscle cramps

Houston Ballet 2016
World-renowned ballet company

houzz

Houzz 2018
Website about home decorating, architecture
and housewares

HUDSON RIVER PK

Hudson River Park 2019
Riverside park and estuarine sanctuary
on the west side of New York City

HUDSON YARDS

NEW YORK

Hudson Yards 2019
New York City multi-use centre

Bedrock Hudsons 2022
Development featuring 1.5 million square feet of office,
retail, food, hotel, residential, event and activated open
spaces in Detroit, Michigan

Henry Wu 2022
Logotype for musician Henry Wu

Hyphen

Hyphen 2017
Global architectural practice

I AM 2020
Anti-Racism Fund zine in service of Black lives
and active allyship

IBA 2018
Internationale Bauausstellung, Stuttgart, Germany

ICC 2022
International Chamber of Commerce – the largest,
most representative business organisation in the world

ICHIBUNS

イチバンズ

The International Center for Photography 2020
A school, museum and archive for visual culture

IDEO 1997
Identity for the product development firm based
in Palo Alto, California, updated from the Paul
Rand original

Igluu 2018
Online real estate platform

'24 ORE

Il Sole 24 ORE 1979
Italian business and financial newspaper

ila 2007
Organic skincare and wellbeing products

ilili 2022
Lebanese restaurant located in the Flatiron district
of New York City

I L° T' C H I"

Impala 2021
Technology-driven travel platform that specialises
in connecting hotels with customers

IMPERIAL

IMPERIAL

Imperial College London 2024
STEMMB university in London

INDEPENDENT

The Independent 2013
One of the UK's national newspapers

Index Ventures 2014
Leading venture capital firm

INDIANA
APOLIS
MUSEUM
OF ART
IMA

Indianapolis Museum of Art 2009
One of the oldest and largest art museums
in the United States

ingui

Ingui 2023
Architecture firm

Inolex

Institute of Contemporary Art, Boston 2019
Contemporary art museum located in the Seaport
District of Boston, Massachusetts

Interactive Week 2000
Newspaper for the web development industry

intrinsic

intrinsic

Intrinsic 2020
Robotics software and AI company at Alphabet

IRENE
FORTE

Irene Forte 2018
Organic Sicilian skincare range

IRENE
FORTE

IRVINGTON THEATER

Irvington Theater 2019
Performing arts theatre established in 1902 along
the Hudson River

Al-Ittihad 2017
Arabic-language newspaper published in the United
Arab Emirates

Jamaica Station 1998
Multi-modal railway station in New York City featuring
a large curved roof

JamesBeard
Foundation

James Beard Foundation 2019
Non-profit organisation supporting the people behind
American food culture

Jane Austen's House 2019
Austen's Hampshire cottage home where the author
wrote six of her most famous novels

JAWHAR

Jawhar 2009
Marrakech luxury hotel, residences and spa

JAWHAR

Jazz at Lincoln Center 2020
New York City Institution for the performance, teaching
and appreciation of jazz.

Jazz at Lincoln Center 2004
New York City institution for the performance, teaching
and recording of jazz

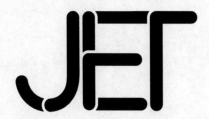

JET: Jewelry, Ethics, Trust 2008
High-end jewellery consulting firm

jigsaw

Jigsaw 2014
American production company created by
Alex Gibney, focusing on documentaries

JOHN LEWIS

JOHN LEWIS

John Lewis 2018
British department store

THE JOSLYN

Joslyn Art Museum 2024
Fine arts museum in Omaha, Nebraska

Joyco 1999
International confectionery group based in Spain

Juzdan

Juzdan 2022
Digital payment platform for Turkish bank, Akbank

JW3 2012
Jewish community centre, London

KaIYO

Kaiyo 2019
Digital platform for buying and reselling high-quality
used furniture

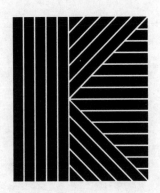

Kanuhura 2004
Luxury island resort in the Maldives

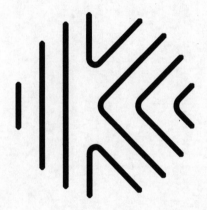

Katerra 2016
Technology-driven offsite construction company
providing fully integrated building services

keap

keap

KEEL.LABS

Keel Labs 2022
Sustainable materials company producing textiles
with aquaculture-based technologies

KeelingAndrew

Keeling Andrew 2023
Fine wine importer based in Bloomsbury, London

Keruen 2014
Kazakhstan retail centre on the Silk Road

Royal Botanic Gardens
Kew

Royal Botanic Gardens, Kew 2015
The largest collection of living plants in the world

khaore

Khaore 2017
Luxury leather goods brand focusing on limited-edition handbags

Kikori Whiskey 2015
Japanese rice whisky brand

KILLING EVE

Killing Eve 2018
British spy thriller television series

K &

EST.
1982

M

King's College London 1992
Prestigious educational institution,
part of the University of London

King's College London 1992

Klang Basel 2014
Music festival in Basel, Switzerland

KPIT

KPIT 2018
Indian multinational corporation that provides
embedded software and product engineering
services to automotive companies

KRUG

Krug 2010
World's greatest champagne

Kubota

Kubota 1989
Machinery manufacturer based in Osaka, Japan

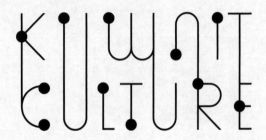

Kuwait Culture 2017
National cultural centre consisting of six museums
and venues

Kuwait Culture 2017
National cultural centre consisting of six museums
and venues

L.L.Bean

L.L. Bean 2008
American apparel and outdoor equipment retailer
founded in 1912

Ladies' Home **Journal**

Ladies' Home Journal 2012
American women's magazine

Landmark 2012
Luxury retail destination in the Central district
in Hong Kong, China

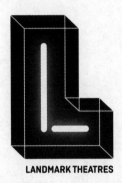

LANDMARK THEATRES

Landmark Theatres 2023
Chain of arthouse cinemas

Lands' End 2003
Direct merchant of classic American apparel

Language 2023
Innovative clothing label

Las Vegas Magazine 2007
Weekly city magazine

Laylow Pictures 2023
Documentary film production company founded by
Academy Award-winning director Ezra Edelman

LBTY.

Lead Development Association 1970s
Conference on electric powered vehicles

Leafs by Snoop 2015
Medical and recreational marijuana-related products

Lenus 2023
Digital platform for health coaches

LeoLogic 1998
French software development company

LIBERTY.

Liberty 2019
Luxury department store in London

L!BRARY

The L!brary Initiative 2012
Programme to build or refurbish libraries in New York
City public schools

LIBR LIBRARY OF CONGRESS ARY

Library of Congress 2018
The library of the United States of America

Libreria 2015
London bookshop by Second Home, designed
by Spanish architects SelgasCano

Lifemark 1999
Providing services to chronically ill populations

ꓥIGHTMATTER

Lightmatter 2020
Industry-leading photonic computing company

Lilly Pulitzer 2023
Chain of women's clothing stores

Litl 2008
Producers of next-generation computer hardware
and software for home use

Little Tokyo 2010
Japanese fast-food chain

Little Green Light 2020
Software company helping not-for-profits fundraise

Lloyd Fonds Capital 2019
Financial company in Hamburg, Germany

LONDON DESIGN BIENNALE

London Design Biennale 2016
Exhibition showcasing global design-led innovation,
contemporary creativity and research

London Fashion Week 2019
Fashion trade show that takes place twice a year
in London

London Taxi Drivers' Charity for Children 2017
Charity run by black cab drivers that helps children
who are most in need

Long Beach 2014
Family resort in Mauritius

LOVEVERY®

Lovevery 2015
Educational products and toys for babies and toddlers
centred on stage-based learning

Lower East Side Tenement Museum 2008
New York City museum that focuses on America's
urban immigrant history

Loyola Marymount University 2019
Top-ranked Jesuit university in Los Angeles, California

Lucas Industries 1976
Manufacturer of electronic components for
the automotive and aerospace industries

Luckyfish 2007
Conveyor-belt sushi restaurant
in Los Angeles, California

Lucy's Fried Chicken 2011
Rock 'n' roll fried chicken restaurant in Austin, Texas

Ludwig Seufert 2016
Family-owned company that creates high-class joinery
and interiors in Germany

LUMINATO

Luminato 2017
International arts festival in Toronto, Canada

MADE IN
CLOISTER

Made in Cloister 2012
Centre for art, performance and craft in Naples, Italy

MADELEINE

Madeleine 2021
Online fashion retailer in Germany

Madison Square Park 2005
Historic New York City park

Maggie's 2017
UK charity that creates centres by world-leading
architects to provide support to people with cancer
and their families

Majid 2017
Comic book anthology, children's magazine and TV
channel in the United Arab Emirates

Maker Park 2015
Industrial reuse advocacy group based in Brooklyn,
New York

Makr Shakr 2014
Robotic bartenders developed
by MIT Senseable City Lab

Mandarin Oriental 1985
International luxury hotels and resorts

Manhattan Records 1984
Recording company based in New York City

The Mansion 2014
Residential real estate development, central London

Mantle 2009
Literary imprint for Pan Macmillan books

Manuvo 2020
Social-lead business using technology and cultural
resources to transform less-privileged communities

ManyClicks 2021
Technology brand that provides real-time
customer feedback

Map Studio 2020
London-based creative agency and publishing house

Mara 2022
Pan-African cryptocurrency platform

Marble Hill 2019
Hillside shopping centre

March of Dimes 1998
Organisation co-founded by Franklin D. Roosevelt
in 1938, providing research, education and advocacy
for infant and childhood health

Marcus 1999
Retail outlet for luxury timepieces

Maremmana 2014
Restaurant in the Maremma, Tuscany, Italy

Marine One 2013
Presidential helicopter competition

M|I|C/A

Maryland Institute College of Art 2007
America's oldest accredited art school

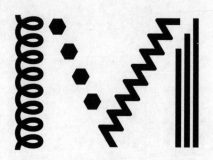

Materials for the Arts 2023
New York City nonprofit providing free materials
to artists and public schools

Matter 2014
Online cultural publication for Medium

מטרי

Matter 2008
London's largest nightclub

Maudie's Tex-Mex 2012
Restaurant chain in Austin, Texas

mayena

Mayena 2012
olding group in Gabon

Mayena 2012
Luxury resort in Gabon

Mellon Foundation 2022

argest funder and grantmaker of the arts

d humanities in North America

MgPt.

Melting Pot 2021
Schmuckmuseum Pforzheim jewellery magazine

**MEMPHIS
ART MUSEUM**

Memphis Art Museum 2023

museum in Memphis, Tennessee

THE MENTAL HEALTH COALITION

The Mental Health Coalition 2020
Organisation that raises mental health awareness

METEOR

ᴛʜᴇ METEOR

The Meteor 2020
Feminist collective dedicated to advancing
gender and racial equity and justice

METROPOLIS

Metropolis 1999
Monthly magazine that examines contemporary
life through design and architecture

METROPOLIS

⋀⋀etropolis

Metropolis by Marcus Samuelsson 2023
Urbane restaurant in lower Manhattan, New York

The Met ropolitan Opera

The Metropolitan Opera 2006
America's largest classical music institution,
located in New York City

MFS Engineering 2019
International façade engineering firm

MICHĒLE

Michéle 1974
Cosmetics brand for Marks and Spencer

Micro-X 1998
Range of high-performance tennis balls from Tretorn

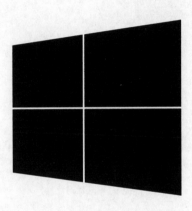

Microsoft Windows 8 2012
Computer operating system from Microsoft

Micrus 1997
Manufacturer of medical instruments and medication-
delivery devices

MIDI 2020
Logo for the technical standard and digital
music protocol

MIHO
美学院

Miho Institute of Aesthetics 2012
Teaching facility on the campus of the Miho Museum
in Shigaraki, Japan

MILLS & BOON

Mills & Boon 2018
The UK's leading publisher of romantic fiction

MindGym 2021
Behaviour-change programmes built
on the latest science

Minneapolis Institute of Art 2016
Art museum and one of Minnesota's largest
art educators

MIT Media Lab 2014
Interdisciplinary research laboratory at the
Massachusetts Institute of Technology

MIT MUSEUM

MIT Museum 2022
The home for permanent and temporary exhibits
exploring the worlds of science and technology

MIT Schwarzman College of Computing 2020
College for computing uniting fields of study at MIT

Modern Art Museum of Fort Worth 2002
Tadao Ando-designed museum that collects and
presents contemporary art

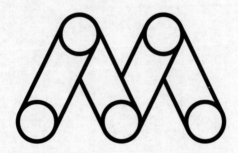

Mohawk 2012
Premium paper manufacturer

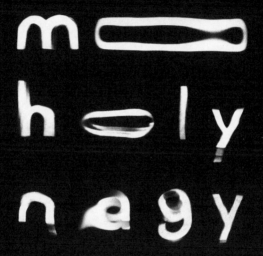

Moholy-Nagy Foundation 2020
The foundation set-up to promote and preserve
the legacy of László Moholy-Nagy's life and work

Monterey Bay Aquarium 2024
Aquarium and ocean conservation centre

MORAVIAN
UNIVERSITY

Moravian University 2021
Private liberal arts university in
Bethlehem, Pennsylvania

The
Morgan
Library &
Museum

The Morgan Library & Museum 2006
Collection of artistic, literary and musical work founded
by J.P. Morgan in 1906

MORSELETTO

Morseletto 2020
Italian marble masonry

MOSS BROS.

Moss Bros. 2014
British menswear brand

MOTH:

MOTH 2020
Bar-quality cocktails in a can

Mothercare 2004
Maternity and childcare retailer

Motive 2021
Integrated cloud-based fleet management
software company

The Motley Fool 2020
Financial and investing advice company

Motoverse 2022
Royal Enfield's motorcycling festival in Goa

Move Dot Com 2012
Online moving resource guide

MOZAMBIQUE RENEWABLES

Mozambique Renewables 2018
Environmental organisation supporting farmers
in Mozambique

Mozart Ways 2004
International network of scholarly and historical sites
associated with the composer

Mozarthaus Vienna 2003
Museum dedicated to Mozart's life and music
in the composer's only surviving apartment

World
Creative
Studio

MTV World Creative Studio 2016
Studio responsible for the global creative output
of the MTV channels

Muraba 2023
Residential real estate developer based in Dubai, UAE

MUSE 2012
Museum of science in Trento, Italy

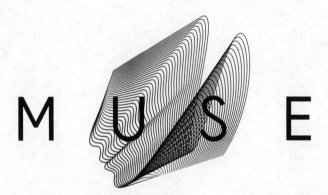

M U S E

Muse 2019
Rolls-Royce art programme, based in the UK

Museum für Film und Fernsehen 2006
German national film and television museum

Museum für Post und Kommunikation 1995
Museum devoted to the history of the postal service
in Germany

Museum of Arts and Design 2008
Contemporary art, craft and design museum
in New York City

THE MUSEUM OF THE CITY OF NEW YORK

The Museum of the City of New York 1997
Presenting the history of New York City and its people

MUSEUM TINGUELY

A CULTURAL COMMITMENT OF ROCHE

Museum Tinguely 2017
Art museum in Basel, Switzerland

**Mushrooms: The Art, Design
and Future of Fungi** 2019
Exhibition at Somerset House, London, that charts
the influence of mushrooms on global culture
throughout history

Myna Snacks 2023
Snack brand offering joy-inducing, satisfying eats

MYTHERESA

Mytheresa 2018
Online fashion retailer in Germany

National Cowgirl Museum and Hall of Fame 2010
Museum in Fort Worth, Texas that celebrates women
who have shaped the American West

National Grid 1989
Formerly the administrative body for the UK's
electricity supply, now a major international energy
utility company

NATIONAL PORTRAIT GALLERY

National Portrait Gallery 1993
The UK's national collection of historic
and contemporary portraiture

The National 2017
Campaign for The National's seventh studio album
Sleep Well Beast

NATIONAL
BUILDING
MUSEUM

National Building Museum 2023
Museum dedicated to the design and creation
of the built world

National
Gallery of Art

National Gallery of Art 2021
America's national art museum, Washington, D.C.

**National Landing Business
Improvement District** 2020
Residential and business district in Arlington, Virginia

NATIONAL SATURDAY CLUB

National Saturday Club 2022
Giving teenagers the opportunity to study
subjects they love at their local university,
college or cultural institution

National Women's
History Museum

National Women's History Museum 2021
Virtual museum that celebrates the history
of American women

Native Instruments 2022
Software and hardware company for computer-based
audio production and DJing

Natural Areas Conservancy 2013
Wildlife protection organisation in New York City

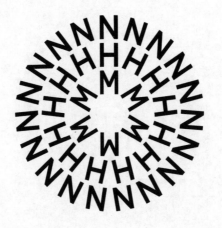

Natural History Museum 2023
World-class visitor attraction and leading science
research centre based in the UK

NAVAN

Navan 2023
All-in-one travel, corporate card and expense-
management solution

ΛELSON&RUSSELL

AROMATHERAPY

Nelson & Russell 2006
Aromatherapy range for Nelsons, Europe's oldest
manufacturer of homeopathic remedies

Nesta 2017
Innovation foundation that backs new ideas to tackle
the big challenges of our time

THE NET–A–PORTER GROUP

The Net-a-Porter Group 2012
Online luxury retailer

NEW
MEXICO
MUSEUM
OF
ART

New Mexico Museum of Art 2020
New Mexico's first art museum, located in Santa Fe

NOMA

New Orleans Museum of Art 2013
Historic art museum focused on painting, sculpture
and the city of New Orleans, Louisiana

NEW PRACTICES
NEW YORK

New Practices New York 2011
American Institute of Architects New York chapter
committee to promote new and innovative architecture
and design firms

The New Republic 2019
Premier US journal of liberal opinion dedicated
to politics, culture and the arts

THE
NEW SCHOOL

The New School 2015
Progressive collection of colleges for the humanities
in New York City

THE NEW SCHOOL
PARSONS

Parsons 2015
Large design college in New York City
(part of The New School)

New Victory Theater 2019
Children's theatre in Manhattan, New York

New World Symphony 2011
Orchestral academy founded by conductor Michael
Tilson Thomas and designed by Frank Gehry in
Miami, Florida

New York City Ballet 2008
America's preeminent dance company

**New York City Economic
Development Corporation** 1992
Promoting economic growth throughout
the five boroughs

New York Jets 2001
'Gameface' graphic mascot for the NFL team

New York Magazine 2004
Revival of the original logo of the city's definitive
weekly magazine

New York Philharmonic 2008
The oldest symphony orchestra in the United States

New York Live Arts 2018
Dance and performing arts centre

The New York Review
of Books

The New York Review of Books 2022
Semi-monthly magazine with articles on literature,
culture, economics, science and current affairs

NewsGuard 2018
Rating platform for news and information websites

niceday®

Nicollet 2016
Large shopping street in Minneapolis, Minnesota

92NY

The 92nd Street Y 2022
150-year-old cultural and community centre
in New York City

92Y

The 92nd Street Y 2008
New York City cultural and community centre

The Ninth 2015
Jun Tanaka's Michelin-starred London restaurant

NISSAN

Nissan 1983
Automotive company

njpac

New Jersey Performing Arts Center 2017
Performing art centre in New Jersey

NLand Surf Park 2016
First inland surf destination in North America

No Man's Land 2017
Magazine with a feminist-centric twist on standard
magazine tropes

Nobrium 1971
Pharmaceuticals brand for Roche

Noguchi Museum 2004
Devoted to the life and work of the Japanese-
American sculptor Isamu Noguchi

noguchi

Nonô 2015
Coconut beach hut in Rio de Janeiro, Brazil

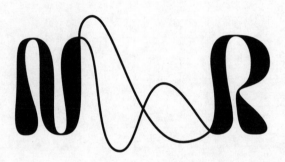

Nordoff and Robbins 2023
The UK's largest music therapy charity

Nubank 2021
World's largest digital bank, founded in Brazil

Numan 2019
Men's health provider in the UK

Nuverse 2021
Game development and publisher brand
by ByteDance

NYC Parks

NYC Parks 2011
New York City Department of Parks and Recreation,
one of the world's largest urban park systems

NYC Votes 2021
Voter-engagement initiative of the New York City
Campaign Finance Board that ensures local elections
are fair, inclusive and open

The Oak Room

The Oak Room 2008
Iconic bar and restaurant located in New York City's
Plaza Hotel

ODD
APPLES

Odd Apples 2021
Photo book celebrating unusual apples, published
with Hatje Cantz

Odd Apples Zine 2018
Large-format photo zine about rare
and curious apples

Odic Force Magazine 2007
Publication about the arts in Austin, Texas

Ohio National Financial Services 1996
Offering financial services and solutions

The Old Kirk 1996
Residential signage for a converted church

THE OLD VIC

The Old Vic 2016
Historic London theatre

OLIVEDΛ

OLIVEDA 2015
Olive tree-based cosmetics

Omaha Performing Arts 2019
Largest arts organisation in Nebraska, encompassing
entities such as the Orpheum Theater and the Holland
Performing Arts Center

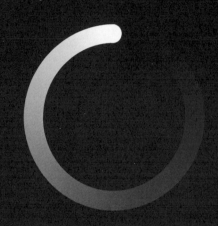

Omicron 2000
Private investment firm

OMNES

OMNES 2020
Sustainable fashion house in the UK

OMNES

OMNY 2019
Contactless fare payment system for New York City's
Metropolitan Transit Authority

O
BEING

On Being 2014
American podcast centred on spiritual inquiry, science,
poetry, social healing and the arts

ONEALDWYCH

One Aldwych 2019
Independent premium hotel, London

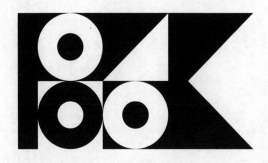

186K Films 2023
Production company founded by Hasan Minhaj

IOO%**design**

100% Design 2007
International design trade fairs for Reed Exhibitions

One&Only

One&Only Resorts 2002
Exclusive collection of international luxury resorts

Onion 2022
South Korean coffee shop franchise

ONMO

Omno
[Publisher information illegible]

bloö

Öola 1988
Confectionery retailer

Opera Ballet Vlaanderen 2019
Leading opera and ballet company
of the Flemish region in Belgium

oppo

Oppo 2015
One of the world's leading smartphone and IoT
technology companies

orby

Orby 2023
Orby restaurant by The Conran Shop Japan

Oregon State University 2017
Public university in Corvallis, Oregon

Orthopädie am Hafen 2019
Orthopedic practice in Berlin, Germany

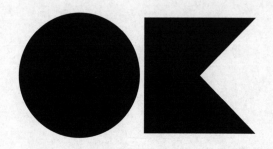

Orthopädie in Konstanz 2023
Orthopedic practice in Konstanz, Germany

Outward Bound Center for Peacebuilding 2007
Education initiative working in regions of conflict

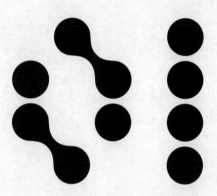

Oxford Ionics 2021
Quantum computing company utilising
trapped-ion technology

0xide

Oxide 2021
Maker of server racks for on-premises
computing infrastructure

OZY Media 2015
American media and entertainment company

Panther Dog 2022
Film production company in Austin, Texas

Pantone 2000
Industry-standard colour-matching system

PAPERLESS

Paperless 2015
Company offering solutions for a paperless office

Parallax Theater 1990
Performing arts collective in Los Angeles, California

THE PARIS REVIEW

The Paris Review 2021
Quarterly literary magazine established in Paris in 1953

PARK LAMAR

Park Lamar 2023
Property development in Dubai, UAE

Parla 2023
Pizza and pasta restaurant in New York City

PathoGenesis Corporation 1992
Company researching the causes of disease

PayPoint 2014
Retail payment systems in the UK

Peach Coffee Roasters 2021
Coffee retailer in Atlanta, Georgia

Peek&Cloppenburg

Peek & Cloppenburg 2022
Chain of department stores

Pelli Clarke & Partners

Pelli Clarke & Partners 2019
International architecture practice

PEN International 2010
Worldwide initiative for writers defending freedom
of expression

PE-A International 2010
Available for sale for within Oceania region
only. No resale.

Penguin Press OH
[illegible]
London And Oxford

Penguin Press 2014
Publishing imprint of Penguin Books, founded
by editor Ann Godoff

Penguin Random House

Penguin Random House 2014
Publishing company with over 250 imprints

Puffin Books 2003
Penguin's imprint for children's books

Pentagram Fives 2020
Music project by Yuri Suzuki and Sascha Lobe

Performing Arts Center of Greater Miami 1999
Complex of theatres and concert halls

Period Equity 2016
Legal organisation that fights for equal rights
for women's health

PERRYELLIS

Perry Ellis 2004
American fashion label

Phaidon Press 1991
Publisher of books on the visual arts

Phenology 2022
Consumer product brand for women centred
on improving the experience of menopause

The Philadelphia Orchestra 2008
Resident orchestra at the Kimmel Center
for the Performing Arts

Philadelphia
Museum of
Art

Philadelphia Museum of Art 2014
Largest art museum and art collection
in Philadelphia, Pennsylvania

Philanthropy University 2015
Online platform that supports a global community
dedicated to locally led, sustainable change

PhilaPhil

PhilaPhil 2015
Friends of the Philharmonie Luxembourg

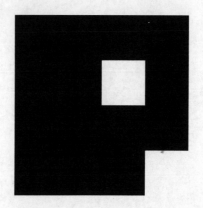

Philbrook Museum of Art 2012
Art museum based in Tulsa, Oklahoma

Philharmonia Records 2022
Record label for the world-class symphony orchestra

|||||||||| | PHILHARMONIE

Philharmonie Luxembourg 2004
The national concert hall of Luxembourg

PHOENICIA

Phoenicia 2011
Leading luxury hotel in Beirut, Lebanon

PHONETICAL

Phoenix Court 2019
Venture funds group, London

PINK FLOYD

Pink Floyd 2016
Record label identity for the celebrated band

Piperlime 2006
Online footwear and accessories retailer,
owned by Gap

Pizza Up 2018
South Korean concept restaurant

Places for London 2023
Transport for London's property company

Platform

Platform 2014
Non-profit organisation and conference dedicated
to entrepreneurial diversity

Platform

Platoon 2020
Platform for musicians to create and distribute music

Plenaire

Plenaire 2018
UK-made skincare brand that encourages emotional
wellbeing and self-care

PLP/ARCHITECTURE

PLP Architecture 2009
London architecture practice founded in 2009

Plus 2005
International not-for-profit coalition simplifying
the management of image rights

POELLATH+

POELLATH 2020
Law firm in Germany

Poetry Magazine 2018
Oldest monthly devoted to verse in the English-speaking world

Polarization Index 2021
Technology metric that grades the divisiveness
of particular topics

POLITAN ROW

Politan Row 2018
Food hall in Chicago, Illinois

Pomological Series 2022
Series documenting the Annual Wild and Seedling
Pomological Exhibition

Pont-Aven School of Contemporary Art

Pont-Aven School of Contemporary Art 2007
International fine arts institution located in the historic
artists' colony of Pont-Aven, France

POPULUS

POPULUS

Populus 2024
Hotel in the cultural and governmental centre
of downtown Denver, Colorado

Port 2021
Biannual style magazine

Portofino Technologies 2022
Financial infrastructure technology startup

PORTRAIT

Portrait 2022
Healthcare collective focusing on aesthetic medicine
and MedSpas

PORTRAIT

Poster House 2017
Small museum dedicated to collecting
and preserving posters

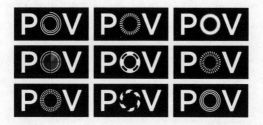

POV 2007
Award-winning documentary film series on PBS

MUSEO NACIONAL DEL **PRADO**

Museo Nacional del Prado 2003
National art museum of Spain

PREQIN

Preqin 2022
Investment data company that provides financial data
and insight on the alternative assets market

A Lincoln

PRESIDENT LINCOLN'S COTTAGE
AT THE SOLDIERS' HOME

**President Lincoln's Cottage
at the Soldiers' Home** 2007
National monument in Washington, D.C., part
of the National Trust for Historic Preservation

PRINCETON
UNIVERSITY

Princeton University 2007
Ivy league university

PRINCIPE FORTE DEI MARMI

Principe Forte Dei Marmi 2011
Contemporary villa hotel on the Tuscan Riviera

Prior Securities 1990
Property developer

Prism 2009
Art gallery in Los Angeles, California

PSi 29 2023
Performance Studies international is a
professional association for academics
working in the field of performance

Public Radio International 1994
American public radio network

The Public Theater 2008
Update of the landmark 1994 identity designed
by Pentagram for the New York City performing
arts institution

Pupatella 2017
Neapolitan pizza restaurant chain

PYER
MOSS

Pyer Moss 2017
Designer Kerby Jean-Raymond's fashion label fusing
the personal and the political

PYER
MOSS

Qasr Al Hosn 2010
Cultural quarter in Abu Dhabi, UAE

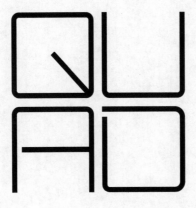

Quad Cinema 2017
Four small movie theatres in one building
in Manhattan, New York

Quarto

Quarto 2023
International publishing group

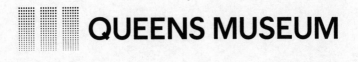

QUEENS MUSEUM

Queens Museum 2012
Museum of the visual arts located in Queens,
New York

Queens Theatre 2015
Local repertory theatre in Queens, New York

Quinnipiac

Quinnipiac 2017
Private university in Hamden, Connecticut and home
of the Quinnipiac Poll

Raaka

Raaka 2018
Single-origin, unroasted dark chocolatier based
in Brooklyn, New York

Radiant Lighting 1996
Distributor of Italian industrial and domestic lighting

RAINBOW ROOM

RAINBOW ROOM

Rainbow Room 2017
Event space at the top of Rockefeller Center

raisin.

Raisin 2015
Fintech democratising global deposit, investment
and pension markets

Rathfinny 2016
Sparkling wine estate in Sussex, UK

Raymond Blanc Organics 2000
Range of organic food products created
with the renowned chef and restaurateur

Rayse.

Rayse.

Rayse 2023
Platform providing clarity and transparency
for real estate agents and clients

RCA UVU 1991
Line of televisions from Thomson
Consumer Electronics

re—inc 2019
Eco-conscious fashion and creative goods brand
founded by USWNT champions Megan Rapinoe,
Tobin Heath, Meghan Klingenberg and Christen
Press, inviting a bold reimagining of our world

Ready Player One 2018
American science fiction action film based
on Ernest Cline's 2011 novel

realme 2018
Global youth-focused smartphone brand
based in China, and one of the world's leading
phone companies

realspace

Realspace 2020
Office Depot's own furniture brand

Red Hat 2019
Technology company in North Carolina specialising
in open source software

reddit

Related Experiences 2005
Entertainment, marketing and sponsorship firm

remission *biome*

Remission Biome 2023
Patient collective exploring novel treatments
for chronic illness

Renaissance

Renaissance 2022
Global educational technology company

THE ~~TORTURE~~ REPORT

The Report 2019
American historical political drama based on torture
investigations following September 11

Republic Records 2017
Popular record label

federal
films

Federal Films 2012
Affiliate of Republic Records

Rescue Now 2023
Ukrainian charity

Research Equals 2021
Open-access publishing site for researchers

Resonate 2015
Annual festival for art and digital culture
in Belgrade, Serbia

Reuters 1968
Classic wordmark for the world news service,
superseded in 1998 by a simpler mark that retained
the familiar 'punched-hole' motif

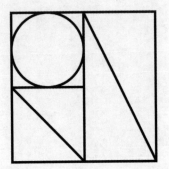

Richard Nicoll 2011
London-born fashion designer whose collections were
characterised by his subtle and modest style

Ricky Williams Foundation 2012
Established by the US football player to support
at-risk children from communities in need

Ridian

Ridian 2022
Cryptocurrency investment platform for consumers

Riotous 2014
Independent theatre company

Rise for Animals.

Rise for Animals 2020
National animal-rights organisation with a mission
to end animal experimentation

THE RITZ-CARLTON

The Ritz-Carlton 2014
International hotel and resort company

Rocco Forte Hotels 2017
Anglo-Italian family-run hospitality collection

ROCKEFELLER
CENTER

Rockefeller Center 2017
Historic civic and commercial centre in the heart
of New York City

The Rockefeller Foundation Centennial 2011
Centenary initiative focusing on innovation
for the next 100 years

Rogers
Stirk
Harbour
+ Partners

Richard Rogers
Mike Davies
Graham Stirk
Ivan Harbour
Andrew Morris
Lennart Grut
Richard Paul
Ian Birtles
Simon Smithson

Avtar Lotay
Ben Warner
Louise Palomba
Tracy Meller
Andy Bryce
Andrew Partridge
Andrew Tyley
Andy Young
Dennis Ho
Dennis Austin
Steve Martin

Rogers Stirk Harbour + Partners 2017
World-renowned architectural firm

Rolls-Royce 2017
Industrial technology company

Rolls-Royce Motor Cars 2020
The British luxury automobile maker

ROHDe

ROHDE 2021
German shoe manufacturer

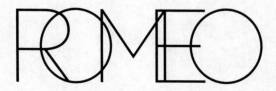

ROMEO 2008
Modern luxury hotel in Naples, Italy

Roole 2021
Twenty-first-century automobile club in France

Rotten Tomatoes 2018
Review-aggregation website for film and television

Rowe Rudd 1968
Stockbrokers

ROXANE GAY BO□KS

Roxane Gay Books 2021
Grove Atlantic's publishing imprint for author
Roxane Gay

Royal Academy 2012
Independent, privately funded institution led
by artists and architects

Royal College of Nursing 1984
Professional association representing nurses
throughout the UK

Royal Institute of British Architects

RIBA

Royal Institute of British Architects 2001
Professional association of UK architects

Royal Mansour 2017
Private medina hospitality in Marrakech, Morocco

RS Group 2020
Thailand's leading entertainment and commerce group

RSA 2011
Royal Society for the encouragement of Arts,
Manufactures and Commerce

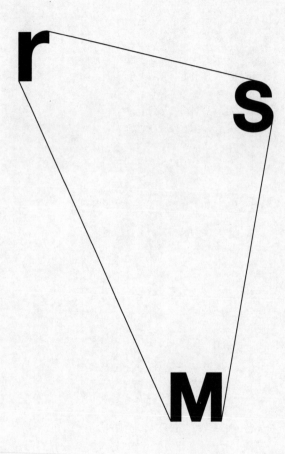

Ruam Samai Museum 2024
Museum featuring contemporary arts with
the largest Chinese and Southeast Asian
crafts collection in Thailand

RubyTuesday

Ruby Tuesday 2007
American chain of casual-dining restaurants

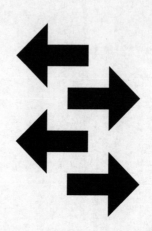

Safe 2012
Insurance brokers in Greece

The Sage Gateshead 2002
Concert hall and centre for musical study

Sainsbury's Skincare 2005
Range of beauty products for a UK supermarket chain

Sakanowa 2022
Japanese website for soccer fans

Saks Fifth Avenue 2007
Iconic New York City retailer

Salt Lake City Public Library 2003
Library system with collections catering to all
members of the community

San Francisco Opera 2006
Second largest opera company in North America

San Antonio Book Festival 2023
Annual book event featuring national, regional
and emerging authors

San Diego Zoo Wildlife Alliance 2021
One of the largest wildlife conservation organisations
in the world

Sandelman Partners 2006
New York City-based hedge fund

Sapora

Sapora 2022
Premium spice, herb and specialty salt brand
in the United Arab Emirates

SARDEGNA

Sardegna 2006
Autonomous region of Italy and the second-largest
island in the Mediterranean Sea

SATURDAY NIGHT LIVE

Saturday Night Live: Season 40 2014
American television show featuring sketch comedy
and musical performances

SATURDAY NIGHT LIVE

Saturday Night Live: Season 48 2022
American television show featuring sketch comedy
and musical performances

SAVOY

The Savoy 2008
Pioneering luxury hotel in London

SCA 1991
Paper and wood products manufacturer

SCIENTIFIC AMERICAN

Scientific American 2023
American popular science magazine

Scott Wilson 1997
Multidisciplinary design and engineering consultancy

Scribner 1995
Simon & Schuster imprint with a distinguished
list of writers

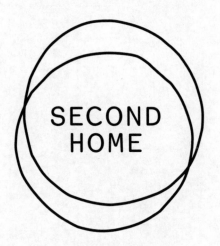

Second Home 2018
Co-working space in London for fast-growing
technology firms and entrepreneurs

Secondmind 2020
AI company that helps automotive engineers design
better cars faster

seekout>

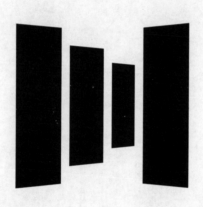

Sekonda 2002
Watchmakers

SELF

SELF 2013
Women's health, beauty and style magazine

seqvoia

Seqvoia 2017
Regtech company from Luxembourg delivering
technological solutions for asset managers and
asset-servicing companies

serif

serif

Serif 2021
Social space to connect LGBTQIA+ communities,
leaders and creatives

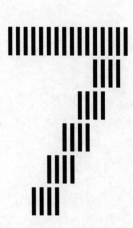

7 World Trade Center 2005
The first tower to be constructed at Ground Zero
in Lower Manhattan, New York

7th on Sixth 1993
Seasonal fashion shows in New York City

Shake Shack 2012
International chain of upscale fast-casual restaurants

Shakespeare Theatre Company 2022
Washington, D.C.'s pioneering theatre company

Shakespeare's Globe 1992
Historic reconstruction of Shakespeare's
original theatre

Sharjah

Sharjah 2023
Destination brand for the Emirate of Sharjah
in the United Arab Emirates

الشارقة

Sharjah 2023
Destination brand for the Emirate of Sharjah
in the United Arab Emirates

SHILLA
STAY

Shilla Stay 2015
Hotel chain in South Korea

Shrüm 2022
Psychedelic mushroom-growing product

Sidwell Friends 2019
Athletics programme at Quaker day school in
Washington, D.C.

SimpliSafe

SimpliSafe 2022
US and UK's leading home-security company focused
on self-installed wireless security

SOM

Skidmore, Owings & Merrill 2015
Architecture firm

the
Skimm'

theSkimm 2020
Digital platform summarising key news stories
in a quick, accessible and conversational format

Skittledog 2022
Imprint from international book publisher
Thames & Hudson

Skolem

Skolem 2022
Full-stack institutional trading platform for DeFi
(decentralised finance with cryptocurrency)

Skyscraper Museum 1997
New York City museum devoted to the history
of high-rise buildings

Slack 2019
Business communications software

SM Corporation 2022
The largest company in the Philippines, specialising
in shopping mall development, retail, real estate
development, banking and tourism

SHI Corporation

Smith+Nephew

Smith+Nephew 1980
Medical equipment manufacturers

Snap Kitchen 2017
Chain of food stores specialising in healthy foods
for a variety of diets

Snoop Dogg Pounds 2017
Smoking accessories and glass pipes

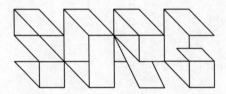

Sorg Architects 2008
Architecture firm based in Washington, D.C.

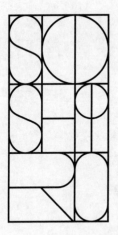

SoShiro 2019
London-based furniture and accessories
collection created, designed, and curated
by designer Shiro Muchiri

Sotheby's

Soufflé

Source 2001
Imprint of Simon & Schuster, publishing non-fiction

SPACE

Space.com 2000
Website focusing on space and space exploration

Spaghetti Recordings 1991
Record label founded by the Pet Shop Boys

Spiritland 2016
London-based restaurant and listening venue that
houses one of the best sound systems in the world

§ SPLASH

Splash Financial 2022
Digital financial platform for refinancing loans

SPYGAME

Spy Game 2018
Interactive spy game

Square Chapel 2017
Arts centre in Halifax, UK

SSG 2023
Sustainability Solutions Group, leading climate change
consultancy creating climate mitigation and adaptation
plans for municipalities, governments, organisations,
utilities and campuses

St Christopher School 2019
Independent school in Hertfordshire, UK

Stanmore Implants 2008
Specialists in skeletal restructuring

STAR ALLIANCE

Star Alliance 1996
World's largest multinational airline alliance

State 2011
Dedicated online opinion network and platform

The Street

TheStreet 2011
Financial media company providing financial news
and stock market analysis

The Street

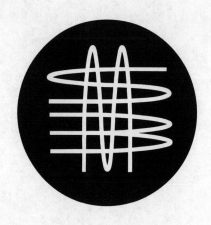

Studio of Martha Burns 1992
Designers of textiles, products and interiors

Studio Louise 2019
Brand and communications consultancy based
in London

STUDIO THEATRE

Studio Theatre 2020
Theatre complex in Washington, D.C.

Success Academy Charter Schools 2015
Largest and highest-performing network of charter
schools in New York City

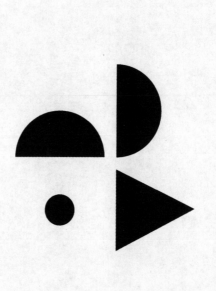

Summerbird 2021
Fast-casual chicken restaurant in Charlotte,
North Carolina

summerill&bishop

Summerill & Bishop 2010
Exclusive kitchenware store in London

Swift

Swift Foods 2018
International food producer

Swiss Dairy 2000
Brand of milk, juice and other dairy-related products

SYSTEM

SYSTEM1

System One 1993
Computerised airline reservation system

THOTEL

T Hotel 2005
Contemporary hotel on the island of Sardinia

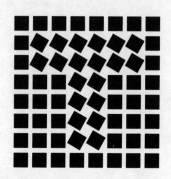

Tactics 1984
Range of high-quality men's toiletries produced
by Shiseido

Taffera Builders 2006
Homebuilders and craftsmen

Teabox 2015
Global tea company from Darjeeling, India

The Technology Partnership 2018
Independent product and technology consultancy
in the UK

Telmo Rodriguez 2002
Spanish winemaker

Tempo 2023
Music production label

10

TenTen 2019
UK government art award: ten years, ten prints

Ten Trinity Square 2014
Hotel, residences and private members' club
in London

Tender Greens 2016
Chain of casual restaurants serving high-quality food

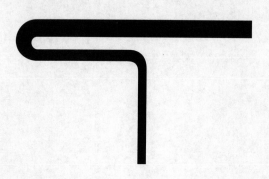

Teravalis 2022
New Arizona community

Ad<ance

Texas A&M Advance 2007
Research magazine for Texas A&M University

Texas Biotechnology 1999
Cardiological research specialist

Texas Book Festival 2017
Annual book event held in and around the Texas
State Capitol

Texas Cultural Trust 2020
Statewide nonprofit with the mission to support
the arts

Texell Credit Union 2022
Credit union in Temple, Texas

Thames & Hudson 2019
Publisher of illustrated books

Thames & Hudson Children's 2023
Children's imprint for the illustrated book publisher

**The Rights
Agency**

TheRiA

TheRia 2019
Sport rights agency based in Munich, Germany

3OROCK

30 Rock 2006
Television comedy created by Tina Fey

Thomas Hayward Auctioneers 1992
Auctioneer and appraisal company

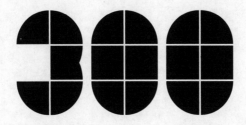

300 East 42nd Street 2019
Office building in Manhattan, New York

THREE
SPIRIT

THREE
SPIRIT

Three Spirit 2023
Non-alcoholic spirit and wine alternatives

TIFFANY & CO.

Tiffany & Co. 2005
Redrawn identity for the renowned luxury retailer
founded in 1837

Tigermilk 2019
South American restaurant chain in France
and Belgium

Time Warner Center 2004
Mixed-use office, residential and retail complex
in New York City

TIMEBASEDARTS

Time Based Arts 2012
Visual effects and colour-grading studio based
in London

Time 2022
South Korean fashion brand

अन्हे

Times Educational Supplement 2011
Publication based in the UK aimed at teachers
and those working in education

tiscali.

Tiscali 2004
Integrated internet access, portal
and e-commerce services

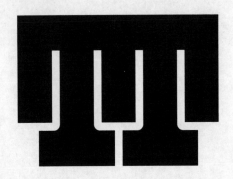

Titletown 2019
Civic park and recreation centre, adjacent to Green
Bay Packers' Lambeau Field

TODΩY

TODAY 2022
Multiplayer web3 world-building game

TOMO

Tomo 2021
Fintech mortgage company

The Tonight Show Starring Jimmy Fallon 2014
American late-night talk show

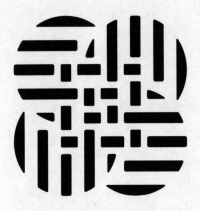

Tony Blair Institute for Global Change 2017
Advisors to governments and leaders on strategy,
policy and delivery

Torch Partners 2018
Corporate financial consultancy for tech firms
in London

Total War: Warhammer III 2020
Real-time strategy videogame developed by Creative
Assembly and Games Workshop, published by Sega

Totem 2023
Product leveraging gamers' time for healthier habits

Touchstone 1999
Simon & Schuster imprint publishing political
and topical non-fiction

Le Touessrok 2007
Luxury resort in Mauritius

Tower Bridge 2018
The symbol of London – a working bascule bridge
and museum

Tractable 2021
Software company that develops AI to assess damage
to property and vehicles

TradingView 2021
Charting platform and social network for traders
and investors

Tragon 2008
Market research and consulting firm specialising
in sensory evaluation

TRAKTOR

Traktor 2022
Product logo for Native Instruments

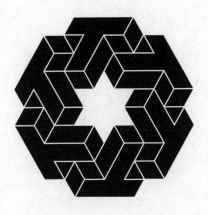

Travel Today 1989
Travel service specialising in tours to Israel

Travis Construction 1986
General contracting company

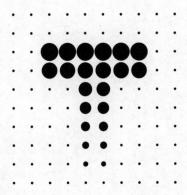

Trevi 1991
Range of premium shower fittings from Ideal Standard

Trio 2002
Cable and satellite television network

TrueCar

TrueCar 2018
Online automobile buying marketplace

TRUSSARDI

truvía

Truvia 2008
Natural no-calorie sweetener

Tulane School of Architecture 2020
Architecture college in New Orleans, Louisiana

21c Museum Hotel 2006
Contemporary art gallery and hotel
in Louisville, Kentucky

Zwice

2wice

2wice 1997
Visual and performing arts magazine published twice
a year

2DADS

2DADS 2021
Independent Canadian brewery

Tyler School of Art and Architecture 2019
Logo for the newly merged college

TYNDARIS

Tyndaris 2012
Financial company

TDC 2012
Movable identity for the Type Directors Club
annual show

UCLA Architecture and Urban Design 2007
School at the University of California, Los Angeles

UNITED STATES HOLOCAUST MEMORIAL MUSEUM

United States Holocaust Memorial Museum 2008
National institution for the documentation, study and
interpretation of Holocaust history and the prevention
of genocide

UniS

University of Surrey 1999
UK university based in Guildford

ual:

University of the Arts London 2012
Institution comprising six colleges around the capital

Untapped 2022
Recruiting platform for candidates looking for jobs
in technology companies

Upworthy 2016
Digital-media company that shares empowering
stories on social media

Urban Green Council 2009
New York City chapter of the U.S. Green Building Council

Urbint 2018
Technology company developing AI-powered solutions
for safe and reliable urban utility lines

URGE 2019
Creative industries collective helping organisations
find radical responses to climate change

USA

USA 2024
Official logo for the Federal Government
of the United States

Utah City 2023
New city in the United States

Vaccine Company 2023
Life-science company focusing on the research,
development, manufacturing and distribution
of vaccines

Le Vendôme 2011
Chateau-like hotel in Beirut, Lebanon

VENN 2017
Skincare brand focusing on science-proven
ingredients and results

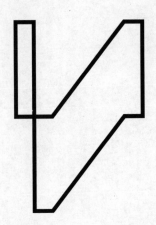

Vention 2022
Leading software development company partnering
with tech leaders worldwide

verizon√

Verizon 2015
Largest wireless communications provider
in the United States

Vibia 2018
Spain's leading lighting company

Victoria and Albert Museum 1989
UK national museum of decorative arts, design
and craft

View 2.0 2011
Proprietary data-visualisation application created
for advertising agency J. Walter Thompson (JWT)

Vilcek Foundation 2024
Foundation and art gallery in New York City
that focuses on the contribution of immigrants
to American culture

VILLAGE

VILLAGE

Village Hotel Club 2015
UK hotel and leisure club network

VIREN

Virgin Family 2023
Online social platform for the Virgin Group

Virgin Money 2019
UK-based financial services brand by Virgin Group

visible

Visible 2017
Mobile service network by Verizon

Vistagen 2021
Pharmaceutical firm

Vivantes

Vivantes 2006
Group of hospitals in Berlin, Germany

Vivo 2007
Tableware collection from porcelain company
Villeroy & Boch

vocativ

Vocativ 2015
Media and technology company using the deep web
to discover stories

vroom

Vroom 2018
Online platform for buying and selling high-quality
used cars

WAITROSE

Waitrose 2018
British high-end supermarket

Walgreens 2005
Leading drugstore chain in the United States

Walker Collection 2017
Collection of bespoke urban hotels

WALKER

Walker Hotel 2017
New York City hotel and restaurant

Waller Brothers 1979
Suppliers of office materials and accessories

|THE WALTERS |
ART MUSEUM |

The Walters Art Museum 2018
Museum and library focused on ancient, Renaissance
and nineteenth-century art and rare books

Warner Bros. 2019
Global film and entertainment company

Warner Chappell Music 2019
Global music publishing company

Warner Records 2019
American record label

The Waterways Trust 2000
Agency promoting the conservation and regeneration
of Britain's inland waterways

Waze 2020
Navigation app with real-time traffic and community-
driven updates

Wbeeza 2022
Electronic musician Wbeeza

Webster Bank 2005
American banking corporation

Welcome to My House 2024
International hospitality consultancy

WELLIN

Wellin Museum of Art 2012
Art museum and teaching facility on the campus
of Hamilton College in Clinton, New York

West Texas Pirates 2020
Youth baseball team in Amarillo, Texas

Westweek 1995
Annual conference for interior designers and architects

#WeThe15

WeThe15 2021
Inclusivity movement for people with disabilities

White City Innovation District 2022
Ecosystem of entrepreneurs

WHITNEY

Whitney Museum of American Art 945
945 Madison Avenue at 75th Street
Manhattan History Gallery

Wien Modern 2016
Music festival in Vienna, Austria

Wildlife Conservation Society 2015
Organisation managing New York City's zoos
and conservation programmes around the globe

THE
WILLIAM
MORRIS
SOCIETY

The William Morris Society 2015
Museum devoted to the Arts and Crafts designer

Willoughby Parking 2014
Automated parking garage

THE WING

THE WING

The Wing 2016
Women-focused social club and co-working space

W/NGS

Wings 2022
Premium credit card for Turkish bank, Akbank

Winter Capital Management 1996
International investment and advisory firm

wirex

Wirex 2018
Borderless digital payment platform for traditional
and digital currencies

Wizarding World 2018
Media company centred on J.K. Rowling's
fictional universe

WNYC 1981
New York City's public radio station

Women's Venture Fund 2020
Investment fund for women-owned businesses

Wonka 2023
Musical film about the origins of Roald Dahl's
Willy Wonka

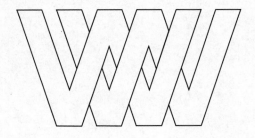

Wood & Wood 1970
Signage manufacturer

Woodgreen 2021
UK-based pet charity that focuses on helping
both pets and their owners

WOOLRICH®

Woolrich 2018
American clothing company

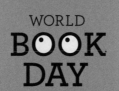

WORLD
BOOK
DAY

1 MARCH 2012

World Book Day 2012
Children's charity

World Chess 2012
Sponsored world championship of chess

World Cup '94 1993
FIFA world championship held in the United States

World Economic Forum 1994
International not-for-profit organisation based
in Geneva, Switzerland

Worldwide Palliative Care Alliance 2008
Global action network that seeks to improve care
at the end of life

Wu Hen 2022
Merchandising for Kamaal Williams

Wyth 2022
Virtual events platform

Yahoo 2019
Pioneering online services provider

Yale School of Management 2008
Yale University's graduate school of business

Yale Engineering 2023
Yale University's School of Engineering
and Applied Sciences

Yashu Farm 2022
Organic regenerative farm specialising in high-quality
vegetable production

Yoto 2019
Interactive, screen-free audio player for children

You Can Now 2014
Training and development partner to growth-
oriented organisations

The Young Foundation 2005
Think tank specialising in policy on social
and community issues

YoungArts 2021
Not-for-profit organisation in Miami, Florida, supporting
high school performing and fine arts

Zeckendorf Development 2007
Real estate development firm

Zeff 2023
Specialist source for wholesale and retail commercial
recycling bins

Zeiträume Basel 2014
Biennale for new music and architecture,
Basel, Switzerland

Zignal Labs 2022
Technology platform that measures the
online conversation

Zipper 2020
Software that helps people make software

Zumpano Studios 1990
Photography studio

First published in the United Kingdom and the United States of America in 2010 under the title *Pentagram Marks: 400 Symbols and Logotypes* by Pentagram and Laurence King Publishing

This edition published in the United Kingdom in 2024 by Thames & Hudson Ltd, 181A High Holborn, London WC1V 7QX

This edition published in the United States of America in 2024 by Thames & Hudson Inc., 500 Fifth Avenue, New York, New York 10110

1,000 Marks © 2024 Thames & Hudson Ltd, London

Introduction © 2024 Pentagram
Captions to the illustrations © 2010 and 2024 Pentagram

Edited by Angus Hyland

British Library Cataloguing-in-Publication Data
A catalogue record for this book is available from the British Library

Library of Congress Control Number: 2024935715

ISBN: 978-0-500-29803-9

Printed by China, by Artron Art (Group) Co., Ltd.

MIX
Paper | Supporting
responsible forestry
FSC® C019910
www.fsc.org